WINDJAMMER

WINDJAMMER

PICTURES OF LIFE BEFORE THE MAST IN THE LAST GRAIN RACE

ERIC NEWBY

NEW YORK · E.P. DUTTON & CO., INC.

Based on the design by Terence Dalley

PRINTED IN GREAT BRITAIN *in Times Roman type* BY JARROLD AND SONS LTD, NORWICH

INTRODUCTION

Most of the photographs which are reproduced in this book were taken while I was serving in the four-masted Finnish barque *Moshulu* of Mariehamn in 1938 and 1939 when she was engaged in the Grain Trade. Great collections of photographs taken on similar voyages by the officers, men, apprentices and passengers exist and some have already been published; but many thousands of unpublished prints and negatives must still be lying, half forgotten, in attics and desk drawers. One day, perhaps, the best of them will be brought together in a series of volumes. I hope so, for no one collection can record fully the life of both the officers and men in the last of the grain and nitrate ships.

Looking back, it seems to me a pity that none of the great photographers who were at work between the wars made a round voyage in one of them. If there had been anything like the number of young professional photographers that there are today, one or two would surely have done so. But the great photographers of the 'thirties were otherwise engaged. The best of them were either busy in Europe recording a way of life that was about to perish for ever, or else they were at the battle front of one of the minor wars that were a prelude to the big one. Besides, few professional photographers could spare the time for such a voyage. A round trip in a sailing ship from Europe to Australia and back took a minimum of eight months and if there were delays in getting a cargo, or the passage itself was a long one, it could easily last a year or more.

And even if he wanted to go there would have been difficulties. Unless he was already experienced in sail he would have had to ship either as an apprentice, a cadet, or possibly as a passenger; and it would have been very difficult to make a single voyage in one of the Scandinavian or German school-ships as a cadet. As an apprentice in one of the Finnish ships he would have had to live in the special accommodation reserved for apprentices, or else in the fo'c'sle. Either way he would have been debarred from mixing with the officers or speaking to the Master unless spoken to. He would certainly have had no opportunity of visiting their quarters—not even to clean them, which was done by the steward's assistant—nor would he have been allowed to use a camera while he was on watch, for it is impossible to work a sailing ship and at the same time take photographs without becoming a dangerous liability to one's shipmates. If, on the other hand, he went as a paying passenger, and many men and women did sail in the Finnish ships before the war as passengers, he would have had to live aft, where he would have been as cut off from the crew as they were from the officers.

I was an apprentice in the *Moshulu*. In an earlier period when British apprentices to the Merchant Marine were required to spend time in square sail before sitting for a mate's ticket, I would have lived with other apprentices, working with the foremast hands but not one of them; but by the time I went to sea the apprentices in most of the Finnish ships lived in the fo'c'sle together with the other boys and the ordinary and able seamen, for the simple reason that apart from ships such as *Herzogin Cecilie*, *L'Avenir* and *Viking*, which had been built as cargo-carrying training ships, there were none with special accommodation for cadets or apprentices. The really big ships, of which *Moshulu* was one, had mostly been built in the 'nineties or early 1900's for the nitrate trade, at a time when steam was already a serious competitor. Although these ships were of immense size, they were built so that they could be handled with the minimum number of men, and the accommodation was proportionate.

Being an apprentice, I took nearly all these photographs during my free watch below; many of them when I was done-in after long hours on deck, at the wheel or up in the rigging. In rough weather it required an effort of will not to go to sleep as soon as one went below, but to turn out again with a camera. For this reason there are few if any pictures in this book of the ship when all hands were called to take in sail, tack or wear her round, bring her to anchor or get her under way from the anchorage. Such moments, as any yachtsman knows, are inimical to photography. A passenger could have recorded them, but there were no passengers in *Moshulu* that voyage.

Although I did not know it at the time, this was to be *Moshulu*'s last voyage in the Australian grain trade, as it was to be for the rest of the Erikson fleet, as well as for most of the German and Swedish ships which took part in the 1939 sailings from the Spencer Gulf. In the autumn of 1938 twelve three and four-masted barques left Europe for Australia—one German barque, *Padua*, sailed from the Elbe to Valparaiso round the Horn in search of a nitrate cargo but she subsequently crossed the Pacific and loaded grain in South Australia with the rest. Thirteen ships sailed for Europe, eleven of them by way of Cape Horn, and by the autumn all of them were back in European waters; but although one or two of them continued to sail during the first year or so of the war, carrying various cargoes, and some even survived into the post-war years, the big Finnish fleet of Gustav Erikson of Mariehamn was dispersed and they never came together again to form the great concourse of vessels which lay in Spencer Gulf, South Australia, in the spring of 1939.

Today there are no more steel, square-rigged sailing ships left trading on the oceans of the world, and it seems unlikely that any that still remain afloat will ever do so again. If any more sailing ships are built for commercial purposes it seems certain that their appearance will be as different from that of the three and four-masted barques that I knew, as the crews which will be employed to man them will be different.

By the 'thirties the grain trade from South Australia to Europe was the last enterprise in which the remaining square-riggers could engage with any real hope of profit, and then only if the owner had an obsessional interest in reducing his running costs. He had to pay his crew, which had to be as small as possible commensurate with safety, as little as possible. He could not afford to insure his ships, most of which he had obtained at shipbreaker's prices; but at the same time he had to maintain them at such a standard of excellence that they were all rated 100 A1 at Lloyd's, or an equivalent classification with other Register Societies. He had to be respected and feared as a hard man over whose eyes no one could pull any wool by the masters whom he employed to sail his ships, for if they were frightened of him then the tremors would be felt by the newest joined apprentice in the whole fleet. Of such stuff discipline is made. An old-fashioned word, but sailing ships do not stay afloat and make passages at the pleasure of committees of seamen.

Such a man was Gustav Erikson of Mariehamn in the Baltic, the last to own a great fleet of sailing ships. He employed no P.R.O.s to improve his image. I never met any foremast hand who liked him—it would be as reasonable to expect a present-day citizen of Britain to 'like' the Prime Minister or the Inspector of Taxes—and in our ship he was known as 'Ploddy Gustav', although most of us had never set eyes on him. The thing that warmed one to him was the certainty that he was completely indifferent as to whether anyone liked him or not. He was only interested in his crews in so far as they were necessary to sail his ships efficiently, and for that reason he ensured that they were adequately and decently fed by sailing ship standards, and that the ships they manned were supplied with enough rope, canvas, paint and other necessary gear to enable them to be thoroughly seaworthy at all times. It is difficult to see what more he could have done. He certainly knew about ships. In fact, he knew as much about his own ships as the men who sailed them. Originally, as a boy of nine, he had shipped in a sailing vessel engaged in the North Sea trade. At the age of nineteen he got his first command in a North Sea sailing vessel, and after that he spent six years in deep-water sail as a mate. From 1902 to 1913 he was master of a number of square-rigged vessels before becoming an owner.

The South Australian grain trade continued to be profitable until 1939. It was a trade that was peculiarly suited to sailing ships for a number of reasons. Spencer Gulf, to which the ships came to load their cargoes is a 180-mile long inlet in the Great Australian Bight. The water is shallow but is navigable by sailing vessels almost to its head. It lies in the very heart of the wheat belt, and behind the little ports on either side of the Gulf the wheat fields stretch away to the horizon. With one or two exceptions these ports are or were of a primitive nature. Some had jetties at which the ships could lie alongside (the one at Port Germein was over a mile in length), but at others they had to lie offshore and load the bags of grain into their holds from lightering ketches, using their own tackle. What kept the majority of steamers away from the Gulf was the absence of any import trade. This meant that any ship coming in to load in the Gulf had to arrive in ballast. It was not a paying proposition for the majority of steamships, and right up to 1939 few of them loaded grain cargoes there.

Although the Great Australian Bight is a dangerous, inhospitable place for ships of any kind, the Gulf itself was in some ways an extraordinarily convenient one for sailing ships. It lies only about 5° north of the most powerful windbelt in the world, the Roaring Forties, and almost exactly at the half-way house for a sailing vessel on a round the world passage from Europe by way of the Cape of Good Hope and the Horn. Maddening delays might be experienced both on entering and clearing the Gulf due to calms, but once clear of Kangaroo Island and out in the Bight it was often not more than a day or so before the Westerlies were picked up for the run to the Horn, over 6,000 miles of sailing.

For the ships engaged in the trade, the normal practice was to sail from Europe about the last week of September or the first week in October in ballast, use the North and South-East Trade Winds in the North and South Atlantic Oceans, and when south of Tristan da Cunha run before the Westerlies in 40S across the Southern Indian Ocean, making what might well be the first landfall of the entire voyage, the lighthouse on the South Neptune Islands at the entrance to Spencer Gulf. Then, unless the port of lading was already known, she would generally sail to Port Lincoln and lie offshore until a freight was fixed and orders were received to proceed to the loading port. Thus ended a journey of some 15,000 sea miles. A good passage outward bound in ballast was around eighty days, although passages of a hundred days and more were common.

It might be weeks, or even months before a freight was fixed. As soon as it was, the ship would sail to the loading port; but first the crew had to get rid of the ballast, shovelling it into baskets, hoisting it out of the hold with the temperature often up in the hundreds and tipping it over the side at the offshore ballast grounds. Few sailing ships had water ballast tanks. It was not possible to jettison all the ballast at once, and one or more trips under sail had to be made to the ballast grounds in the interval of loading the cargo which was itself frequently interrupted by the strong breezes which spring up quickly in the Gulf and blow for a day or so at a time. Loading was a long enough business without these delays. The bags of grain which had been brought down from the back blocks had first to be put into the lightering ketches and then brought out to the ship and loaded. A 3,000-ton barque could take more than 60,000 sacks of grain. With such arrangements a twelve-week turn-round between arrival in the Gulf and departure was not uncommon.

The normal date of departure for Europe varied between the last week in February and the last week in March, although a ship which had been lucky enough to secure a cargo of timber from Finland to East Africa on the outward voyage or a charter to load guano at one of the lonely islands in the Indian Ocean for New Zealand, might arrive at the Gulf later and leave later. Sailing for Europe in February or March and making a really good passage of a hundred days for the 14,000-mile voyage by way of the Horn, the ships usually reached Falmouth or Queenstown, the order ports, some time between the first fortnight in June and the middle of July. It could take half as long again but the charterer was not worried; providing it was kept dry, grain was not a perishable cargo and whoever happened to own it at any particular time, for it often changed hand several times during the voyage, was getting free warehousing for his cargo while it was at sea. Some of the smaller and more ancient ships and cargo-carrying cadet-ships would go by way of the Cape of Good Hope, but although about 1,200 miles shorter it was much slower and they rarely made the passages which the Cape Horners were capable of.

Nearly all the Erikson ships discharged their cargoes in the United Kingdom, and when they had done so they would either go into dry dock at the port of discharge, or go back to Mariehamn, their home port, in the Aland Islands in the Baltic and dry dock at Copenhagen when outward bound in the autumn. By that time their hulls would be very foul, having been afloat for nine or ten months and having sailed some 30,000 sea miles.

By the late 'thirties the numbers of ships taking part in the trade had more or less stabilised. In 1921 about sixty loaded grain for Europe at Australian ports. They included French, British and Scandinavian vessels. In 1929 only fourteen loaded. That year the last barque to sail under the British flag, the *Garthpool*, was lost at the Cape Verde Islands and the five-masted Danish cargo-carrying cadet ship *Kjøbenhavn* went missing with all hands somewhere in the South Atlantic. By 1933 the number had risen to twenty-one, of which seventeen were Erikson ships, two were German and two were Swedish.

Some of the best and most powerful ships that Erikson possessed were originally German owned and built for the Chilean nitrate trade. The sailing ship trade in nitrate, which was used extensively before 1914 as a fertiliser, barely survived the first war. It persisted into the 'twenties but this was virtually the end of it, apart from two German barques *Padua* and *Priwall* which loaded nitrate into the late 'thirties. Until 1914 Chile had supplied ninety per cent of the world's nitrate needs; but the war brought about such an increase in the production of artificial nitrates, that by 1935 Chile was supplying only fifteen per cent of the world's consumption. Germany, whose fleet of sailing ships was one of the two greatest carriers of nitrate in the world, was foremost in the development of synthetic nitrates, the production of which, together with the opening of the Panama Canal, which enabled liners to devote part of their carrying space to nitrate, ended the sailing ship's participation in the trade for all practical purposes.

For sailing ships the nitrate trade was one of the toughest in the world. The voyage from the Channel outward round the Horn in the teeth of the prevailing westerly winds was hard and dangerous. The nitrate ports themselves on the western seaboard of Chile, on what was known as 'The Flaming Coast'—Tocopilla, Pisagua, Caleta Buena, Mejillones, Iquique, Antofagasta and Taltal, to name some of the principal ones—were mostly inhospitable places, lacking in amenity. Some of them were nothing more than shanty towns and collections of adobe huts with a population that was a hotch-potch of native stevedores whose job it was to load the ships with the nitrate from lighters, agents, sailors who had deserted their ships, owners of halls in which the *fandango* was danced nightly, and pimps and prostitutes; places still remembered, nevertheless, by old sailors with great nostalgia. The anchorages were often dangerously exposed, either to the exceptionally violent winds known as 'northers', which sprang up with little warning, or to tidal waves which were the aftermath to the sometimes violent *terremotos*, the earthquakes which frequently convulsed the littoral. Unless a vessel could find shelter from them it would either founder or else be thrown several hundred yards up on the shore where it would remain as a sort of monument.

Navigation on the coast was difficult. In opposition to the northerly winds was the coastal current which had a strong northerly set. It was so strong that if a ship made its landfall to the north of its destined port, no uncommon thing, especially for ships which had crossed the Pacific from Australia with a cargo of coal for a Chilean port, it might take a month to reach its destination against it.

The coast itself was, and still is, horrible. Hot, dusty, treeless, earthquake-prone and backed by desert and desiccated, waterless mountains; behind it, in the unimaginable interior, were the nitrate mines.

By 1914 two great fleets of sailing ships, one French, the other German, more or less dominated the nitrate trade, that of Antonin Dominique Bordes et Fils of Bordeaux and Ferdinand Laeisz's 'Flying P' line of Hamburg. Dom Bordes, a firm whose origins went back into the 1840's, really began to take a serious interest in the nitrate business in the 'eighties, when they started buying and commissioning iron and steel barques and ships, most of which were built in Scottish yards. They were beautiful ships which could be readily identified at sea by their graceful lines and black and white painted ports. By 1914 they numbered forty-six with a carrying capacity of over 160,000 tons; but by 1918 enemy action had accounted for twenty-two of them.

Up to that time the French merchant marine had had the advantage of a government subsidised navigation bounty which amounted to Fr.1.70 a gross ton for every thousand miles sailed or steamed, as well as a generous building bounty. Under their benign protection France's sailing ship tonnage increased while that of other nations declined, but the danger of the subsidies was that it provided owners with an unnatural protection and when they were withdrawn at the end of the war Dom Bordes was unprepared to compete without them and the fleet simply melted away.

Laeisz's 'Flying P' Line—the names of all their ships began with the letter P— was, like Dom Bordes, largely built up in the 'eighties and 'nineties; but unlike the French, the Germans were not protected by subsidies. By 1914 Laeisz's nitrate fleet was the most efficiently run fleet of sailing ships in the world. In its heyday it included the two most powerful sailing ships ever built, the five-masted steel barque *Potosi* and the five-masted ship *Preussen*. In 1890 Henderson's of Partick had built the first five-masted steel barque, the *France*, for Dom Bordes, 3,800 tons, which could carry 49,000 square feet of sail, and in 1892 she was a then record seventy-one days from the Channel to Valparaiso. In 1895 she ran from Iquique to the Channel in seventy-nine days with 6,000 tons of nitrate under hatches. But good as the *France* was her performance was not as good as that of *Potosi* and *Preussen* under their great captains.

Potosi was built by Tecklenborg on the Elbe in 1895. On her maiden voyage under Captain Hilgendorf she sailed from Ushant to Iquique in sixty-six days. Carrying 6,000 tons of nitrate, she ran home from Iquique to the Lizard in sixty-eight days as against *France*'s seventy-four days from Iquique to Dunkirk. In 1902 the same yard launched the *Preussen*. She was a five-masted ship, carried a crew of forty-seven, 8,000 tons of cargo, spread 59,000 square feet of sail, and had $18\frac{3}{4}$ miles of running rigging. There was nothing freakish about either ship except their size and performance. Both had the capacity with winds of the right strength and in the right quarter to storm along at sixteen knots, and with a favourable fresh gale, force 8, both ships could and did average over thirteen knots.

Over the years in which they sailed for Laeisz, the passages they made read more like those of express trains for their consistent excellence than those of sailing ships sailing out and home to Chile round the Horn twice a year. Some of their best performances, were *Potosi*, Channel to Valparaiso, fifty-five days and fifty-nine days (twice), and Iquique to the Channel, fifty-seven; *Preussen*, Channel to Iquique, fifty-seven, Iquique to the Channel, sixty-eight, and Tocopilla to the Channel, fifty-six.

But it was not by the performances of these two egregious ships that the achievement of the Laeisz fleet must be measured; but rather by the sheer consistency of the whole fleet. Ships like *Pommern*, *Pamir*, *Passat* and *Peking*, to name only a few, all made passages of under seventy days from the Channel to Valparaiso, and equally good ones home. And not all the Laeisz ships were German built. *Ponape* was built in Italy, *Pommern* and *Parma* were British built (*Parma* years later made the fastest post-war passage to Falmouth from Spencer Gulf, eighty-three days, in 1933); but it was German captains who sailed them and it was Laeisz who brought the loading arrangements at the nitrate ports to such a state of efficiency that the turn-round of their ships was the fastest of all the ships engaged in the trade.

Laeisz lost their whole fleet to the Allies in 1918, but Ferdinand Laeisz succeeded in buying back a number of his ships from countries which had no idea of how to use them effectively—*Peiho*, *Parma*, *Passat*, *Pinnas*, *Pamir* and *Peking* were bought back, but only temporarily. The post-war shipping slump and the economic collapse of Germany rendered their dispersal imperative to Laeisz, and many of them went to Gustav Erikson and other Scandinavian owners.

Nevertheless Laeisz launched two more barques in the post-war years. *Priwall*, laid down in 1916 by Blohm and Voss of Hamburg, but not proceeded with because of the war, was completed in 1920. *Padua*, built by Tecklenborg at Wesermunde, was launched in 1926. These were the two last commercial, four-masted barques to be built, and the last of their kind which are ever likely to be built. Long before the war Laeisz had become convinced that, in spite of the remarkable performances put up by their two five-masted vessels, the most effective ship and the easiest to handle for the nitrate trade was a steel four-masted barque of around 3,000 tons, three-island construction, steered from the raised bridge-deck amidships and fitted with brace and halliard winches.

Passat, *Pamir* and *Peking* were all built to this specification and so were *Padua* and *Priwall*. Both these barques were worthy of their predecessors; *Padua* made passages of sixty-four, sixty-two and seventy-one days outward bound from the Channel to Corral in the nitrate trade, and in 1938 ran from Mejillones to the Channel in sixty-nine days. In 1938 *Priwall* made the westward passage round the Horn from 50S South Atlantic to 50S South Pacific in five days, fourteen hours, which has never been equalled by any sailing ship, either clipper or steel barque. But their most remarkable achievement was in 1936 in the grain trade, when both ships left the Elbe on the same tide and arrived together in Spencer Gulf sixty-six days out. *Padua* and *Priwall* and ships like them were the final flowering of centuries of maritime experience. Such a ship was the *Moshulu* of Mariehamn. Good as they were, neither *Padua* nor *Priwall* ever did better inward bound from Australia than *Moshulu*'s ninety-one days in 1939, although *Priwall* equalled it in 1935; and they did have far bigger crews than any Erikson ship.

Moshulu was originally named *Kurt*. She was built, together with a sister ship, *Hans*, by William Hamilton of Port Glasgow for G.H.J. Siemers of Hamburg and they were both designed for the nitrate trade.

The shipping firm of Siemers, one of the oldest in Hamburg, had become involved in the nitrate trade about the same time as Dom Bordes and Laeisz. They were not as large as either, but by 1910 they owned six fine sailing ships as well as steamships. The latter were mostly engaged in the carriage of *quebrachos* to Europe. The bark of the *quebrachos*, a weird tree which grew in the forests of Paraguay, was brought down to the coast from the interior and was then shipped to Europe where it was used for medicinal purposes.

Up to the time that *Hans* and *Kurt* were laid down, the company had bought its ships rather than built them. They owned *Edmund* (ex *William Tell*), a 3,000-ton four-masted steel barque built in 1891 by Ramage and Ferguson at Leith, who later built the five-masted *Kjøbenhavn*; *Susanne*, a 2,000-ton three-masted iron ship built in 1885 and lost on the Scillies in 1911; *Herbert*, a 2,000-ton four-masted steel barque, built by Russell of Greenock in 1892, and which was possibly the best performer; and the 3,000-ton four-masted barque *Egon*, built by Rodger of Port Glasgow in 1892. *Egon* was the sister ship of *Parma*. *Hans* and *Kurt* were both steel four-masted barques and both were, for all practical purposes, identical.*

They were the last two four-masted steel barques to be built by William Hamilton and were among the last to be built on the Clyde. They were built there because, at that time, they could not have been built as cheaply in a German yard to such a high standard of excellence. Completed they each cost £36,000, and announcements of their launching appeared in Lloyd's Weekly Shipping Index. It would be interesting to speculate on how much they would cost today. They were both launched in the spring of 1904.

The two barques were just over 3,100 tons gross, and they were 335 feet long

---

* For a detailed description of the construction of *Hans* and *Kurt* see *Windjammers Significant*, J. Ferrell Colton; J.F. Colton & Co., Flagstaff, Arizona, 1954.

between perpendiculars. Their cargo capacity was around 5,000 tons and deep-loaded they drew about 26 feet. Their extreme breadth was nearly 47 feet. They were of the three-island construction favoured by the Germans with short fo'c'sle head decks forward, 85-feet well decks forward of the raised 65-foot amidship bridge deck, 130-feet long after-well decks, and short poops, only 20 feet long. Both ships were fitted with bilge-keeps to discourage rolling. They were both very sharp fore and aft and, for their size, their run was very fine. The steering was from amidships and was connected with the steering gear under the poop by cables which ran aft through sheaves in the deck. There was a pair of emergency wheels under the poop which could be manned if the steering cables parted. The hold was in two parts, an upper hold and a lower. The upper hold was 8 feet high and 288 feet long. The lower hold 18 feet 9 inches high amidships and 303 feet long. Both upper and lower holds were pierced by four cargo hatches and openings and more than 200 solid $4\frac{1}{2}$-inch steel pillars tied the main deck to the between deck and the between deck to the floors below —down there in the main hold with all these columns it was like being in a cathedral.

The standing rigging, shrouds, backstays and forestays, was of steel wire set up with rigging screws; the running, rigging sheets, tacks, braces, halliards, clew and buntlines, downhauls, brails, etc. were either wire, chain, hemp or manilla. Altogether some 300 lines were belayed to belaying pins on the pin rails on deck, or else led to cleats or massive bitts.

The masts, yards, bowsprit, in fact all the top hamper, were of steel except for the five feet or so of mast below the trucks, the gaff booms on the aftermast, the jigger mast, all of which were of Oregon pine. The three square-rigged masts which towered 198 feet above the keel were hollow and tapered and built of overlapping $\frac{3}{8}$-inch steel plates, the lower mast and topmast being in one piece. Above them were the topgallant and royal masts. All four masts had a uniform rake aft of about $2\frac{1}{2}°$ which was about half what was customary in similar ships. The fore, main and mizzen masts were each crossed by six yards. From top to bottom they were the royal yards, the upper and lower topgallant, the upper and lower topsail and the course sail yards, eighteen in all. Three of the yards to which the sails were bent on each square-rigged mast were fixed yards and three were hoisting yards, the royal, the upper topgallant and the upper topsail. These were raised in tracks on the forepart of the masts by means of halliards. The royal yard was raised by hand or capstan power, the two heavier yards by worm drive winches worked by hand. In addition there were special brace winches for bracing the topsail and course yards, which were operated by turning cranks. Petrol winches were used for loading cargo. There were also seventeen fore-and-aft sails—five headsails, three staysails set on the royal, top-gallant and topmast stays between each of the masts, and three more on the jigger mast—a triangular gaff topsail which hauled to the masthead, an upper spanker between the gaff boom and the upper spanker gaff and a lower spanker on the spanker boom itself. Both these last two sails were set loose-footed. This was an arrangement peculiar to German nitrate barques which made for greater ease of handling. With all this sail set *Kurt* and *Hans* carried over 45,000 square feet of canvas; but in practice such a press of sail was rarely set, royal staysails being not often bent.

With all this canvas and top hamper the weight aloft was enormous. The course yards alone were more than 95 feet long and each weighed over five tons. The course sails themselves—foresail, mainsail and mizzen—weighed over a ton each and much more when they were wet.

Both ships, when they belonged to Siemers, had black and white painted ports, but by the time *Kurt* had become *Moshulu* and Erikson bought her, she had black topsides with white upper works on the bridge deck, and it was difficult for anyone who was not an expert to distinguish her from many of the ex-Laeisz ships. It was only the apparent shortness of her fo'c'sle head deck and the extreme shortness of her poop which marred her otherwise fine appearance, that enabled her to be distinguished from *Passat* and *Pamir*. These, the absence of any safety netting under the bowsprit and her masts which had less rake to them, were distinguishing marks.

A month after *Kurt* was launched and rigged she left the Clyde for Port Talbot in South Wales. There she loaded coal and sailed for Chile on June 21st, arriving at Pisagua on September 29th, 100 days out. Something must have delayed her because, according to Lloyd's Shipping Index, she did not sail from Iquique until November 18th, 1904, from where she made a very slow passage of over 100 days to the Channel, being off Beachy Head on March 7th, 1905. This was the first of seven outward voyages with coal from Welsh ports to the West Coast, nine voyages from Chile to Germany with nitrate, four ballast passages from West Coast ports to Newcastle, New South Wales, four passages from Australia to Chile loaded with coal and three passages from Hamburg to Santa Rosalia, Mexico, with coke and patent fuel for the copper smelting mines. The majority were not particularly outstanding, but in 1911 she was sixty-nine days from Cardiff to Valparaiso, which was good considering that she was carrying something like 5,000 tons of coal. Some of the Laeisz ships outward bound carried a comparatively light general cargo. (When *Preussen* went ashore in 1910 under the cliffs near Dover, after being hit by a storm, she was carrying a cargo which included cement, coke, barbed wire, brown paper, pianos and school children's slates.) *Kurt*'s best time to the Channel was seventy-seven days from Tocopilla under her second captain, Wilhelm Tönissen, in 1910; but she made some slow passages as well. Her best outward passage was sixty-eight days, deep-loaded with coal, from Cardiff to Valparaiso in 1911. What she was really capable of was demonstrated in 1909 when, also under Tönissen's command with a cargo of 4,920 tons of coal on board, she ran from Newcastle (N.S.W.) to Valparaiso in thirty-one days fourteen hours, 6,376 miles of sailing, during which she twice ran 300 miles between positions, a performance that has only been excelled on the same passage by two other vessels, the four-masted iron ship *Wendur*, 2,046 tons, and the iron four-masted barque *Loch Torridon*. Both these ships sailed together from Newcastle on January 1st, 1896, and reached Valparaiso twenty-nine and a half and thirty days later, the difference being seven hours. *Kurt* had to wait thirty years before she would ever run 300 miles and more in a day again.

Hans was less fortunate than *Kurt*. The first to be launched in February 1904, she left Port Talbot on April 28th with a cargo of coal; but by May 31st she was in Falmouth, having suffered an explosion in the after hold while off the Azores, which damaged the beams and deck set-up. She was sent to the Clyde for repairs and eventually arrived at Iquique in December. In 1906 she broke her tow in the Elbe and went aground, but was got off the next day with only slight damage. In 1910, while off the Dutch coast, she again broke her tow and went ashore on Terschelling but again got off without serious damage.

In August 1914 both *Kurt* and *Hans* were at Santa Rosalia, on the western shores of the Gulf of California in Mexico, a place as unattractive and desolate as any nitrate port but popular with sailors, to which they had gone with cargoes of coke and patent fuel for the copper smelting plant. *Hans* was on her eleventh voyage, *Kurt* her tenth. There *Hans* lay with eleven other German sailing ships, at first sheltering from the war and later interned from 1914 to 1920, when they were all bought by the Robert Dollar Company of San Francisco through the Reparations Committeee in Washington. *Hans* was re-named *Mary Dollar*. She was sailed to San Francisco, where she remained rotting gently in the Oakland estuary until 1935, when she was re-named *Tango* and turned into an offshore gambling ship. In 1941 she was re-rigged as a six-masted schooner, the second largest six-masted schooner ever commissioned. The next year she left Astoria, Oregon, with a cargo of lumber for South Africa by way of the Horn, a passage of 103 days. In 1943 she was sold to a Portuguese owner in Durban and after various misfortunes ended her life in Lisbon in 1946, where she was dismantled. A slow, sad end for one of the most powerful sailing ships ever built.

Kurt's active life was not longer, but it was much less ignominious. When war was declared in 1914 she sailed from Santa Rosalia for Portland, Oregon, where she was supposed to load lumber for Europe. Instead she laid up in Astoria, where she remained until she was seized when the United States entered the war in 1917. She was then re-named *Dreadnought*, but the name was subsequently changed to *Moshulu* when it was found that many of the new names given to German ships were already in the American Registry. The name *Moshulu*, a North-American Indian name, was given her by Mrs Woodrow Wilson, the wife of the President, who took upon herself the arduous task of selecting indigenous American names for ex-enemy ships. It was she who bestowed the name *Monongahela* on the unfortunate German barque *Dalbek*.

Between October 1917 and May 1920 *Moshulu*, now ex-*Dreadnought*, ex-*Kurt*, was owned by the United States Shipping Board and for them she made seven voyages from the West Coast of North America to Manila and back and two to Australia, to load wool and chrome. While outward bound in 1920 on the second voyage to Australia she was sold to the newly constituted Moshulu Navigation Company of San Francisco. From Australia she sailed with coal to Manila and then to San Francisco where in August 1921 she was sold to the Charles Nelson Co. of San Francisco for $29,505. She was laid up for nearly a year in San Francisco, until June 1922, when she took a cargo of lumber from Everett, Washington, to Capetown in eighty-nine days and sailed back from Port Elizabeth to Port Angeles in ballast in 101 days. From January 1924 to April 1927 she was laid up in the Oakland estuary, where so many other sailing ships ended their days; but in June that year she sailed from Portland, Oregon to Williamstown, near Melbourne, with timber in eighty-eight days by way of the Pacific. She was then seventy-five days from Geelong to Port Angeles, where she was laid up again, first in Lake Union and then Winslow, near Seattle, from February 1928 until March 1935, by which time no one thought she would ever sail again. She was still one of the finest steel barques afloat and when Erikson bought her he did so in preference to any other on the West Coast on the advice of Boman, one of his trusted captains whom he had sent to the United States for the purpose of buying a strong four-masted barque to make up for the loss of the full-rigged ship *Grace Harwar*, which had just been scrapped. He paid $12,000 for her, a remarkable bargain even by his standards.

He had her towed to Victoria, British Columbia, where she was cleaned and re-rigged and re-fitted at Yarrow's yard at Esquimalt Harbour by Boman and thirteen officers and men who were sent out from Finland for the purpose. It was a tremendous undertaking, but when it was completed *Moshulu* was un-doubtedly one of the strongest sailing ships left afloat. Her hull, apart from a certain amount of pitting, was as good as it ever had been. She was furnished with a complete set of sails from one of the Alaska Packers' barques and she was re-classified 100 A1 at Lloyd's. On September 29th, 1935, she sailed for Port Lincoln in ballast with a crew of only twenty, five of whom were inexperienced American boys, which allowed only six foremast hands in each watch. She went by way of the Pacific and was seventy-six days on passage. She loaded grain at Port Victoria and sailed in February 1936 for Queenstown with a crew of twenty-eight and made passage of 112 days. This was not a bad performance for what was virtually a maiden voyage. Of the seventeen ships that sailed from Australia in 1936, only four made passages of under the hundred days. They were all Erikson ships. *Herzogin Cecilie* was eighty-six days, the best passage she ever made under the Finnish flag, *Pamir* was ninety-eight, *Passat* was eighty-seven and *Pommern* ninety-four. The two Swedish training barques, *Abraham Rydberg* and *C. B. Pedersen*, were 130 and 117 days, *Killoran* 120, *Lawhill* 118, *Parma* 117, *Viking* 116 and *Winterhude* 117. This was a disastrous year for grain ships. *Herzogin Cecilie* went ashore in the Channel while on passage from Falmouth to Ipswich where she was to discharge her cargo, and eventually became a total loss; *Parma* was so badly damaged while docking in Glasgow that she never sailed again, and *Ponape* was so strained in severe weather off the Horn and in the South Atlantic that she was sold to shipbreakers.

That autumn of 1936 *Moshulu* was 99 days to Port Victoria from Elsinore and 102 days to Queenstown from Port Adelaide. That year *Passat*, *Pommern*, *Pamir* and *Archibald Russell*, all comparable ships, beat 100 days. Any modern windjammer that beats a hundred days can be considered to have made a first-class passage.*

In the autumn of 1937 three Erikson ships loaded timber cargoes in the Baltic for African ports: *Moshulu*, *Archibald Russell* and *Lawhill*. *Moshulu* was seventy-six days to Lourenço Marques from Copenhagen, *Archibald Russell* eighty-seven. Both barques were thirty-seven days in ballast to Port Victoria across the Indian Ocean.

Eleven ships took part in the 1938 sailings and *Moshulu* was a slow 122 days to Queenstown. It was a slow year. *Winterhude* was 165 days, *Archibald Russell* 130, *Killoran* 128, *Penang* was partially dismasted in the Tasman Sea and the *Admiral Karpfanger*, ex-*L'Avenir*, went missing in the Southern Ocean on her first voyage under the German flag with a crew of sixty including forty cadets. Erikson had sold her the previous year to the Hamburg-Amerika line for £17,500, nearly six times as much as he had paid the Belgian Government for her.

*The best recorded passage from Spencer Gulf is that of the British steel barque *Swanhilda*— sixty-six days from Wallaroo to Queenstown in 1899, a remarkable performance which came within a few days of equalling that of the wool clippers which began their voyage on the east coast up to a thousand miles and several days' sailing to the east of Spencer Gulf.

Moshulu discharged her cargo at Belfast and sailed for Port Lincoln in ballast on October 18th, 1938. She was eighty-two days on passage. It was the second best ballast passage of the year after *Pommern*, which was seventy-eight days from Belfast to Port Victoria. *Moshulu*'s best day's run in twenty-four hours was 315 nautical miles, probably the best day's run she ever made in ballast.

Thirteen ships took part in the 1939 sailings, *Moshulu* sailed from Port Lincoln for Queenstown on March 2nd, 1939, and was thirty days to the Horn, well over six thousand miles sailing. On March 24th, running the easting down in 50S, 170W, with the wind WSW and a heavy sea, she ran 296 miles in twenty-three and a half hours (a day noon to noon in these high latitudes is only about twenty-three and a half hours), in all square sail for the first part until five in the evening and carrying upper top-gallants until five the following morning. On the previous day she made 282 miles. On March 29th, in 51S, 136W, with the wind NW, force 6–8, she logged 114 miles between noon and 8 p.m., at times running fifteen knots with the lee rail under water.

She was fifty-five days to the Line and it seemed possible that, having done this, she might beat *Parma*'s eighty-three-day voyage from Port Victoria to Falmouth in 1933. In that year *Parma* had been thirty days from Port Victoria to the Horn and fifty-six to the Line; but unfortunately *Moshulu* now suffered baffling calms and headwinds in the North Atlantic and eventually she was ninety-one days to Queenstown. It was the fastest passage of the year. She just beat the German barque *Padua*, which was ninety-three days to Falmouth. *Pamir* and *Passat* were ninety-six and ninety-eight days. *Winterhude*, *Killoran* and *Lawhill* 134, 139, 140 respectively. This was the last of what pedants refer to as 'the so-called "Grain Races"', though what else they could be called with the highly competitive instincts of the masters, officers and crews it is difficult to know. *Olivebank* was lost this year on passage to the Baltic after discharging her cargo at Barry. The first casualty of the war, after having made a passage of 119 days to Queenstown, she was sunk in the German minefield south-west of Esjberg with the loss of her captain and thirteen of her crew.

But this was not the end for *Moshulu*. From Queenstown she was towed to Glasgow and after discharging her cargo she sailed for Gothenburg in ballast. On October 7th, 1939, with Captain Sjögren still in command, she sailed from Gothenburg for Buenos Aires, which she reached fifty-five days out. There she loaded grain. She sailed for Europe on January 26th, 1940, and was sixty-five days to Farsund. Norway was already occupied by the Germans and on arrival she was seized and ordered to Kristiansand to discharge her cargo. She reached the port on May 22nd. This was *Moshulu*'s last voyage in cargo.

The only member of the crew who remained aboard her was the sailmaker,

John Sömmarström; the rest returned to Finland, which was at war with Russia. She remained at Kristiansand until March 1942, when the Germans had her towed to the Oslo fjord. There, at Horten, she was rigged down and the masts and yards taken ashore. They were subsequently destroyed by bombing, thus making it unlikely that she would ever go to sea as a barque again. After this the sailmaker returned to Finland. From Horten she was taken in tow for Kirkenes and went ashore on passage but was re-floated. Eventually she reached the Lofoten Islands, where she remained at moorings until September 1947, when she broke them and stranded in a gale. In May 1948 she was re-floated by two salvage vessels. Her hull was then bought by a Miss Jacobsen of Narvik for nearly twice as much as Erikson had paid for her in 1935. She was towed to Bergen and there sold to another Norwegian buyer, Trygve Sommerfelt. She was used as a grain store in Stockholm from 1948 until 1952.

In 1952 she was bought by Heinz Schliewen, a German shipowner who had already bought *Pamir* and *Passat* from Belgian shipbreakers. He intended to re-rig her completely and use her as a cargo carrying cadet ship; but unfortunately the cost was prohibitive and in 1953 he sold her to a Swedish firm together with the strange, hybrid, auxiliary topsail schooner *Carl Vinnen*. Finally, in 1953, *Moshulu* was sold to a Swedish firm to be used once more as a grain store and on November 16th, 1953, she was again towed to Stockholm.

What induced young sailors to go to sea in the Erikson ships in the 'thirties? Principally, the Regulations governing the Finnish Merchant Marine, which laid down that a candidate for second officer must spend three years in sail before going ashore to a State Navigation School. Until Hitler came to power, numbers of Germans sailed before the mast in order to get in the time required by their own government, but it then became obligatory for them to serve their time in German ships. The other Scandinavian countries had similar arrangements. Even the English Channel pilots had to have a year in sail in order to be qualified to handle a square-rigger. To qualify, if they had not already done so as apprentices in the last British sailing ships, they either served in *Waterwitch*, a little barquentine built in Poole in 1871, or else made a round voyage with Erikson.

The Erikson crews were not large. In 1937–8 *Moshulu* carried a crew of thirty-three, more or less what her accommodation was designed to carry. The following year, when I was in her, it was twenty-eight—it should have been twenty-nine, but an American apprentice fell down the hold before she sailed from Belfast. It consisted of the Master, three officers, a steward, a sailmaker who was also the bos'n, a blacksmith or 'donkeyman', a carpenter, a cook, a steward's boy, three able seamen, six ordinary seamen, four apprentices and five *Jungman* or boys who were the equivalent of apprentices, but Finnish nationals.

Apprentices were bound by the Conditions for the Acceptance of Apprentices in Finnish Sailing Vessels. These stated that they had to be not less than sixteen years of age and of strong constitution. Two doctors' certificates were required, one of which said that the candidate would not be harmed by the work of a seaman. Another from a clergyman had to state that the boy was of good moral character. In addition, his parents had to pay a premium to the owner of £50 for a year or a round voyage, whichever was the shorter. If he died a pro-rata repayment of premium was made. He had to supply his own gear and he was paid 100 Finmarks a month until 1938 when it rose to 150 (about 10/-). A *Jungman* received about twice this. Later, when an apprentice or a *Jungman* became an ordinary seaman, which he did after a round voyage, he received about 500 Finmarks, but he had to put forward a security of 5,000 Finmarks to be held by the owner in case he deserted in a foreign port, which could be very expensive for the owner and was not an uncommon happening.

An A.B. got about 600–700 Finmarks a month, the sailmaker about 800 (the sailmaker in *Moshulu*, who was an exceptionally experienced man, got about 1,400), the steward about 2,000, the mates from 1,200 to 3,000 and the Captain about 4,000 (£20). Not much for such a lonely position of responsibility. The youngest of the crew was about sixteen, the majority between sixteen and twenty, the officers were in their twenties, the Captain in his thirties. The oldest was the sailmaker, who was nearly sixty.

This was the size of the crew that *Moshulu* had been designed to be handled by. American wooden clippers of the 1850's, such as Donald McKay's *Sovereign of the Seas*, 2,421 tons, carried a complement of 106—Master, four officers, two bos'ns, two carpenters, two sailmakers, three stewards, two cooks, eighty seamen and ten boys. With such huge crews they could take in and set sail at the whim of the Master, and this must be taken into account when the performances of some of Erikson's ships, some of which were fifty years old, are compared with them. The American soft-wood clippers soon became fatigued by hard driving, and many of their best performances were on their maiden voyages.

The *Sobraon*, a British clipper in the Australian passenger trade, carried a crew of sixty-nine; an iron full-rigger of the 'seventies, the *British Ambassador*, carried a crew of forty-one plus six apprentices; the huge German five-masted *Potosi*, a crew of forty-four: Master, three officers, two bos'ns, sailmaker, carpenter, blacksmith, cook, steward, sixteen A.B.s, fourteen O.S. and three apprentices.

Half the foremast hands in *Moshulu*, the year I sailed in her, were first voyagers and although many of them were country boys with strong constitutions, all the newcomers—including myself—found the work very hard at first, even with the aid of brace and halliard winches, particularly that involved wearing or tacking ship which we did frequently during the first few days and nights in the Irish Sea.

The work of handling the great acreage of sail was very heavy. Thirty-four days out from Port Victoria, two days after we had passed the Falkland Islands on the homeward voyage, we started bending a complete suit of old patched fair-weather canvas for the tropics in order to save wear-and-tear on the strong stuff, sending the storm canvas down on gantlines. Sail changing was done always when entering and leaving the Trade Winds, four times on a round voyage. While we were engaged in this work it started to blow hard from the south-east; then it went to the south, blowing force 9 and then 10 and 11 from the south-south-west, when the mizzen lower topsail blew out. This was followed by a flat calm and torrential rain. In the middle of the night a Pampero, a terrible wind that comes off the east coast of South America, hit the ship, when it was practically in full sail. Because the Captain knew his job we only lost one sail, the fore upper topgallant.

In these twenty-four hours the port and starboard watches, eight men to a watch, took in, re-set, took in and re-set again twenty-eight sails—the heaviest of which weighed $1\frac{1}{2}$ tons—a total of 112 operations—bent two new sails and wore the ship on to a new tack twice, an operation which required all hands, including the cook, to perform it and which took an hour each time it was done. The starboard watch were unlucky, having to spend eleven consecutive hours on deck. This was by no means uncommon. Strangely enough, I look back on the time I spent on the *Moshulu* with the greatest pleasure.

MOSHULU, *ex* DREADNOUGHT, *ex* KURT

four-masted steel barque; 5,300 tons d.w., 3,116 gross, 2,911 net. Built by Wm. Hamilton, Port Glasgow 1904. Owners: G. H. J. Siemers and Co., Hamburg, The Charles Nelson Co. Inc., San Francisco, and Captain Gustav Erikson, Mariehamn.

Kurt setting out on her maiden voyage from the Clyde, May 1904

Moshulu in Belfast Lough, September 1938

It was a cold October morning when I first saw the *Moshulu*. She was lying in the York Dock at Belfast, and even the scaffolding in the shipyard at Harland and Wolff's seemed insignificant by comparison. At that time she was the biggest sailing ship in the world

As I went up the gangplank my legs trembled under me at the thought of going aloft, as I knew I must

Almost as soon as I was on board with my gear the Second Mate sent me aloft in the main rigging— 'Op in the rigging'. The first stop was at the main top, a roughly semi-circular platform, braced to the mast by steel struts called futtock shrouds, which was 82 feet above the heel of the lower mast. The next stretch to the cross trees, a triangular construction was 46 feet; the royal yard, the highest of all when mast-headed in its working position was 162 feet above its load line, and the truck was 198 feet above the keel. The last six feet to the mast cap up which the Second Mate made me shin was just bare pole

Plate 31 is a photograph of unknown origin showing *Moshulu* in June 1936 discharging a cargo of grain in Cork (Cobh)

She was still discharging her cargo, after a poor passage, 120 days from Port Victoria to Queenstown, 62,183 bags of wheat, 4,878 long tons, which she had loaded at 41s 3d a ton in Spencer's Gulf in April, and the stevedores weighed the sacks as they came up out of Number 1 cargo hatch on the foredeck

Every morning while we were in port we went over the side to chip rust and red lead the shell plating

When the cargo was discharged we warped up to a lonely quay where we took on 1,500 tons of ballast, sand, part of an old house and two dead dogs which the men on the dock included 'as a joke', for the outward voyage to Australia

Then we went into a graving dock. Here you could see her lines. Unlike most square-riggers built at the end of the nineteenth century *Moshulu* was not slab-sided. She had a very fine run with a hollow entrance and departure aft

Each of the two bower anchors which were fitted with stocks weighed about two-and-a-half tons

We sailed for Port Lincoln in Spencer's Gulf, South Australia on the afternoon of October 18, 1938. The graving dock was filled and the men on the dockside raised the caisson and hove it out clear

A single tug took us up the Lough towards the Irish Sea. It was a
cold, dreary afternoon

In the last of the light we began to make sail

The Mates chose their watches. I found myself in the port watch

Both port and starboard fo'c'sles were amidships, under the bridge deck on which the wheel and the charthouse were situated. They were both approximately 20 feet long and 13 feet wide. Each had twelve berths, only ten of which were occupied, the remaining two being loaded with sea chests and gear. In the centre was a long table. The 10-lb can of margarine contained the ration for ten men for one week. It never lasted

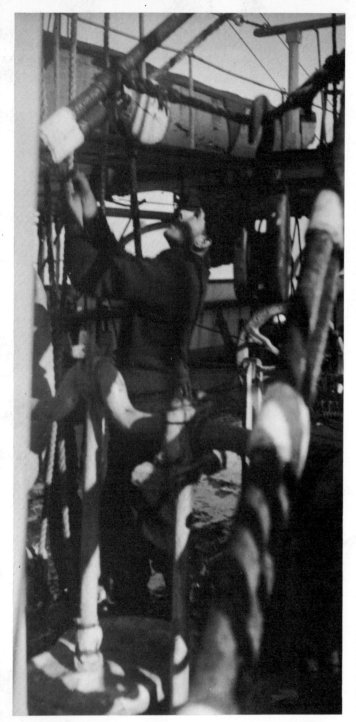

It took us five days to get into the North Atlantic by way of the North Channel. Now the ship's work began. Bestriding the gulf between the officers and the crew was the Sailmaker, John Sömmarström. At that time he was fifty-eight years old and had spent forty-three of them at sea, always in sail. He spoke fluent English with a Scots accent and was very well-read

The canvas he worked with was Webster's 24-inch standard flax from Arbroath. The main course sail (*left*) measured 88 feet on the head and it weighed over a ton. There were no reef points and there was therefore no reefing

On the night of October 24 the wind came up from the sw., and *Moshulu* ran 13 knots under upper topgallants

Two '*Matros*' (Able Seamen) putting a seizing on the main stay. A double stay, it led from thumb cleats above the main top to a pair of rigging screws shackled to lugs in the deck. Like all the other standing rigging it was of steel wire. The sail set on it was the main topmast staysail

The starboard watch tail on to the mizzen royal halliard to raise the yard. The mizzen course sheet is led to the capstan

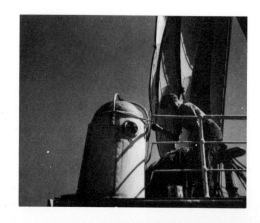

Saturday morning. Washing down the paintwork on the main deck
(*Right*) Painting one of the lighthouses on the fo'c'sle head which
protected the port and starboard lights

The half door under the main bridge deck amidships leading to the port fo'c'sle and to the galley. We dreamt constantly of food

Apprentice Newby doing *Backstörn*—washing-up—in the starboard fo'c'sle, using a half kerosene can of hot sea-water. There were three fo'c'sles, including one amidships where the 'daymen' (carpenter, donkeymen, sailmakers) had their meals. *Backstörn* was most difficult in the fo'c'sle in which the watch below was. Most of its members played a noisy variant of whist called *Bismarck*. Fifty minutes was allowed for washing-up and everything had to be spotless whatever the weather. The job lasted a week. Cleaning the lavatories was far preferable

(*Above*) A Finnish *Jungman* (boy) and a Danish apprentice
(*Below*) Danish apprentice from the schoolship *Danmark*

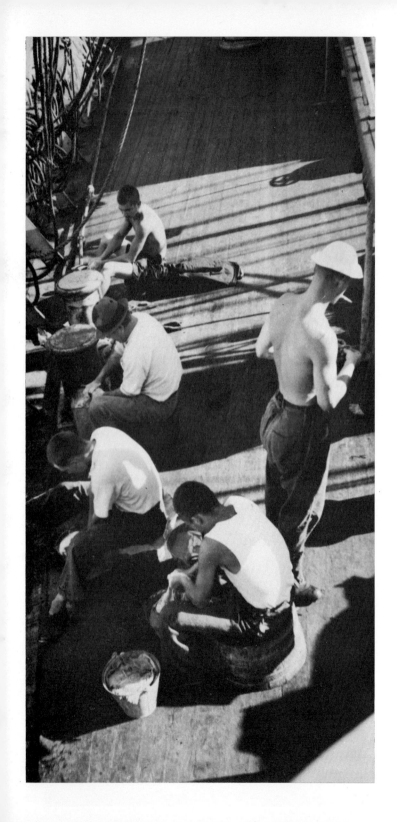

Twelve days out on October 30, we were in 40°N., 16°W. Between noon on 25th and 27th the wind was strong from the west and we sailed 496 miles. On Sunday, now that there was no more fresh water to spare we washed our clothes in sea-water on the foredeck, and cut one another's hair

The *Timmerman* (Carpenter)

Twenty-two days out, in 27°N., 20°W., we began to send down the storm canvas and bend old, patched, fair-weather sails in order to conserve the good stuff. A complete suit of thirty-one sails cost, at that time, about £2,500. The halliard winch in the foreground was one of two abaft each of the three square rigged masts for raising and lowering the upper topsail and upper topgallant yards

The starboard watch send a sail aloft in the fore-rigging

Bending the mizzen lower topgallant to the jackstay with robands
made from rope yarns

Twenty-four days out we picked up the North-East Trades in 23°N., 19°W., about 150 miles off the coast of Rio de Oro. Here the mainsail is bent and the man on the weather yardarm is hauling out the head of the sail and reeving the head earing to a hook on the yard

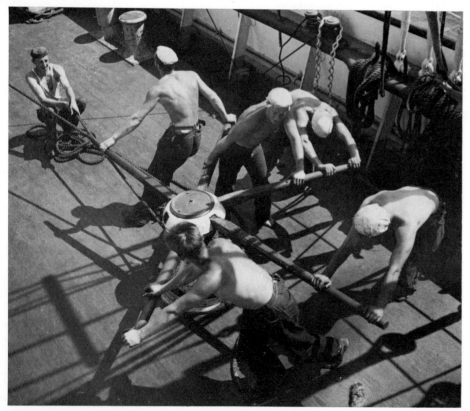

Sending aloft and bending a royal, 160 feet up. The jackstay to which the head of the sail is secured runs along the top of the yard. In some cadet training ships, unlike *Moshulu*, there was another parallel to it which served as a hand-hold. Underneath the yard is the footrope or 'horse'. Footropes were sometimes tested by being stretched between two capstans and being beaten with an iron bar. If they broke they were replaced

The bridge deck seen from aloft in the mizzen rigging (*facing page*)

(*Left*) The mainmast with all square sail set. The two fore-and-aft sails are the main topmast and topgallant staysails. There was provision for royal staysails but they were never bent while I was in *Moshulu*, except for the fore royal staysail

This blew out in a tornado and was never replaced. The four headsails seen here are the fore topgallant staysail, the outer and inner jibs and the fore topmast staysail

Captain Michael W. Sjögren. A huge man, for five years previously he had commanded the ex-British four-masted barque *Archibald Russell*

Danish apprentice at the wheel on the amidships bridge deck. The twin wheels were connected with the steering gear under the poop by wire cables which ran in sheaves. Sometimes these cables broke in heavy weather, and then a similar pair of auxiliary wheels under the poop had to be connected to the steering quadrant, and manned —very quickly

In the warm weather the fo'c'sles became uninhabit-
able because of the bed bugs which swarmed in
them in thousands. We made hammocks from old,
rotten canvas which we begged from the Sailmaker.
In the working watches by day, besides working the
ship we chipped rust and red-leaded

The Assistant Sailmaker with a small model of *Moshulu*

There was a lot of model-making. The Second Mate's was the biggest and best

The Sailmaker with a model of *L'Avenir*, in which he served four years after Gustav Erikson bought her from the Belgian Government. As the *Admiral Karpfanger* she was lost with all hands in the Southern Ocean in February 1938. (*Below*) Able Seaman, ex *Herzogin Cecilie*

The Sailmaker was a great man. He put heart into us when we were done in

Apprentice overhauling buntlines on the fore course. The buntlines were used for drawing the sail up to the yard for furling. They ran through wooden thimbles on the front of the sail and were fastened to cringles in the foot with a special, un-jammable buntline knot. When the sail was set and sheeted home, enough line had to be hauled up through the bunt-blocks on the yard and stopped with easily breakable seizings to leave some slack at the bunt and prevent chafing

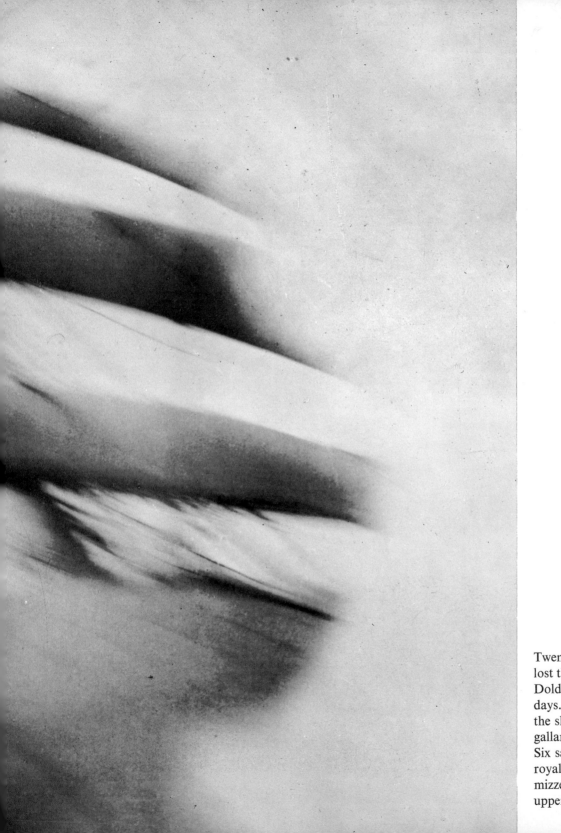

Twenty-eight days out, in 9°N., 21°W., we lost the North-East Trades and entered the Doldrums in which we remained for five days. The following morning a tornado hit the ship, catching her in full sail with topgallant staysails and fore royal staysail set. Six sails blew out: the foresail, the mizzen royal, the fore royal staysail, the main and mizzen topgallant staysails and the gaff upper topsail

The remains of the foresail. All that morning we were bombarded by violent rain squalls

Swaying a new foresail aloft

(*Left*) Going aloft to bend a new mizzen royal. It rained and rained and we collected a lot of fresh water in the scuppers which we poured into a tank on the fore deck

Thirty-two days out, we picked up the South-East Trades in 4°N., 22°W. In the previous twenty-four hours we had only sailed 76 miles. Now, in the next four days, we sailed 931

We crossed the Equator thirty-four days out, in longitude 29°w.
The initiation ceremony was pretty rough. Those who had not crossed
before were given a coat each of red lead, stockholm tar and white
paint, and the *Sydkryss*—the Southern Cross—was cut in their hair
down to the scalp and picked out in green paint

We were then given a pudding to eat made of dough, nutmeg and engine oil. Anyone who resisted seriously was given a terrible going-over. Afterwards we were issued with a certificate, and *Akvavit* was issued to all hands. Everyone got rather drunk and there was some sporadic fighting. We got the worst of the paint off with paraffin and sand

The greatest difficulty had been to find two enamel bowls of equal
size to upholster Neptune's wife

83

Fortunately, the next day was a Sunday. We lay around licking
our wounds

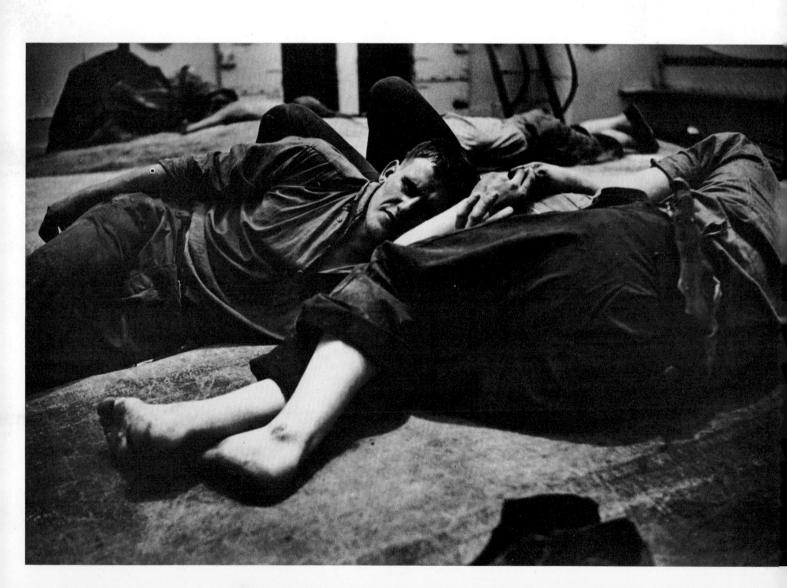

. . . And playing *Bismarck*

The foredeck seen from the fore yardarm. The rectangular construction is the 'donkey house' which contained the donkey engine which
was sometimes used for sending sails aloft, but only in port.
Next to it, covered with sails, is number one cargo hatch

Thirty-six days out the Brazilian Penal Colony of Fernando Noronha was abeam, some 80 miles to starboard. By now all the experienced seamen in the ship had been taken off watch and had been made 'daymen'—either helping the Sailmaker to mend sails or else reeving new running rigging or splicing ratlines

Apprentices and boys were sent aloft in bosun's chairs to paint the shrouds or else to grease the wire braces with a mixture of oil and tallow. These were terrifying jobs as the greatest crime was to drop paint or grease on the deck

Forty-two days out we started to send down the tropical canvas and to bend storm canvas once again. On this day, November 29, we passed close to the uninhabited island of Trinidad, 680 miles off the coast of Brazil; but we did not see it. Instead we saw the first albatross, and the following day the *Carl Vinnen*, a five-masted, auxiliary semi-schooner inward bound, probably from Montevideo to Hamburg. The crew were bending tropical sails

We lost the South-East Trades in 23°s. Two days later *Moshulu* began to go

From noon to noon on December 3 and 4 with the wind first ENE., Force 3 to 4 and later NE., Force 6, carrying royals in the first twelve hours and lower topgallants in the second and running to the SE. she logged 333 sea miles and made 315 between observed positions. Between noon and midnight on December 4 she logged 168 miles

Taking in upper topgallants

On the morning of December 5, we re-set the upper topgallants and the main and mizzen courses which we had taken in at ten o'clock the previous night. Between noon on the 4th and noon on the 5th *Moshulu* ran 316 miles. In the evening, just as the sun was setting we made our first landfall, Inaccessible Island, 20 miles wsw. of Tristan da Cunha, 1,700 miles w. of the African mainland, 1,800 miles E. of the coast of South America and 1,320 miles sw. of St Helena

The summit of the Inaccessible Island was 6,700 feet high and its
cliffs rose to a thousand feet. It was inhabited by a species of flight-
less bird, *Atlantisia Rogersi*, and penguins. On the water there were
thousands of seabirds

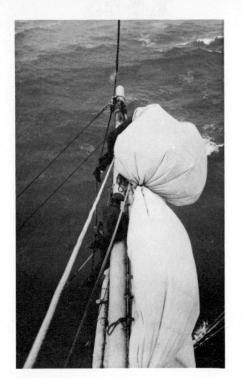

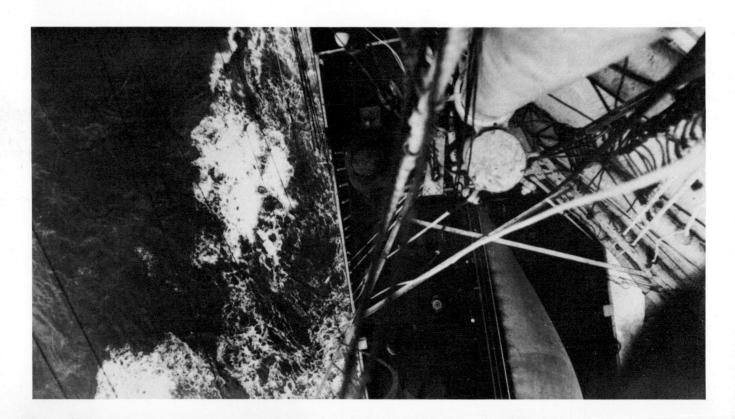

On December 11 we picked up the West Wind in 39°s., 9°E. On December 13 we crossed the longitude of the Cape of Good Hope in 40°s., fifty-six days out

(*Left*) Furling the main royal

(*Right*) Sheeting home the fore topgallant staysail

(*Left*) Taking in the fore topgallant staysail. The steel bowsprit was 69 feet long and there was no netting under it as there was and still is in most surviving sail training ships. This was the most dangerous place to work in the whole ship

(*Right*) The main bridge deck amidships; characteristic of the big German barques which were built for the nitrate trade at the beginning of the twentieth century

(*Left*) The starboard watch trimming the yards on the main mast

(*Right*) At the main Jarvis brace winch

On the foredeck

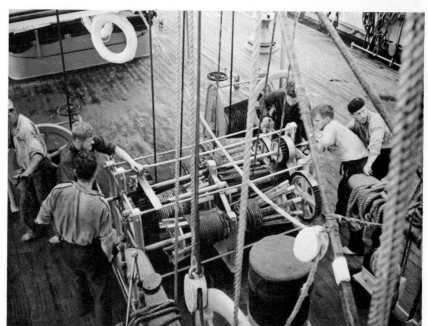

One of the three Jarvis brace winches. Course yard braces wound on to the forward drums, nearest the camera, lower topsail braces to the centre ones, upper topsail braces to the aftermost drums. Topgallant and royal yard braces were not operated by winch but were rove through blocks on each of the after masts to the deck where they were belayed to pins on fife rails

In the Roaring Forties albatross were with us constantly. Purely out of curiosity, not realizing that we might drown them, we angled for them with a hollow triangle of brass to which a piece of stockfish was sewn supported by a cork float. The birds caught their beaks in the trap and were hauled on board. They were always sick when we hauled them in, and after admiring them on the poop we used to throw them back into the sea where some of them perished, being unable to take off again

We sailed 4,713 miles across the Indian Ocean in twenty-one days, always to the s. of the fortieth parallel. On Christmas Day we were in 43°s., 75°e., sixty-eight days out. On the 77th day we entered the Great Australian Bight and on January 7 at four in the morning we made a landfall at Cape Catastrophe to the west of the entrance to Spencer's Gulf. After beating about to leeward for a day and a night we got a favourable slant and ran in past the South Neptunes. At three in the after-noon we anchored by Boston Island, 8 miles off-shore from Port Lincoln, eighty-two days out from Belfast, having sailed 15,000 sea miles

Passat was already at anchor. She had arrived on
December 24, ninety-one days from Copenhagen
106 and was still waiting for a cargo

The next day *Lawhill* arrived eighty-five days out from Birkenhead

(*Below*) *Moshulu* seen from the boat in which we rowed over to visit *Passat*

It was a week before we were allowed ashore. A terrible wind blew down the Gulf from the deserts of the interior and the shade temperature was 114°. With no money, for the Captain, prudently, had not paid us, we were allowed to row in the 8 miles to Port Lincoln; by this time the wind had dropped

(*Right*) The Captain's launch

Passat at the ballast grounds

After two weeks at this exposed and inhospitable anchorage, during which *Moshulu* frequently dragged her anchors, news came that Clarkson's, the London agents of the Erikson fleet, had secured a freight of 27*s* 6*d* a ton for the *Moshulu*

In the hold the temperature went up to 120° and the two dead dogs somewhere in the ballast began to make themselves felt

We worked for another six days digging ballast out of *Moshulu* (on the fifth day we found the dogs)

After six and a half days with half the ballast still in her we walked
the anchors out of the ground and made sail for Port Victoria on
the other side of the Gulf

The concourse of commercial square riggers at Port Victoria in February 1939 was the last the world will ever see: *Olivebank*, *Pamir*, *Pommern*, *Viking* and *Moshulu*—all four-masted barques

Pamir and *Moshulu* at Port Victoria

Pommern loading from a ketch at Port Victoria

(*Right*) Figurehead of *Pommern*

Pommern sailing in from the ballast grounds

Viking at Port Victoria

'Port Veek' as the boys from the ships called it was a
one-street town. Beyond it was Australia

Kneebone's was the café to which most of the crews went when they got ashore. We all had one thing in common: we were practically penniless and permanently hungry

Fortunately the inhabitants were extremely hospitable

There was grain everywhere in Port Victoria. It was the reason for the existence of the place

Bagged, it was run out on a light railway on to the jetty where the ketches waited to take it out to the ships

Some of us were tempted to desert into the ketches as the pay was very good

(*Right*) *Moshulu* with a sandstorm blowing up astern

Viking was the first to sail. She left Port Victoria on February 16. We were a month at Port Victoria, sometimes it blew Force 6 and loading had to be abandoned. By March 9 the lumpers had put 59,000 sacks of grain into her; 4,875 long tons

Pamir sailed on March 8 from Port Victoria. *Passat* on the 9th and *Lawhill* on the 15th, both from Port Lincoln; *Pommern* and *Olivebank* from Port Victoria on the 20th; *Winterhude* from Port Germein on the 22nd; *Kommodore Johnsen*, the four-masted German auxiliary barque from Port Lincoln on the 26th; the German *Padua* from Port Lincoln on April 3. *Abraham Rydberg* had already left Port Germein on February 18, and *Killoran* finally sailed from Port Lincoln on July 13. Both these last two came home via the Cape of Good Hope. That year, 1939, thirteen ships sailed from the Gulf. *Moshulu* (*right*) sailed on Saturday March 11. Her destination Queenstown for orders

With a fair wind from the N. and the anchors aweigh a man was put over the side to strop and secure them in turn to the hook of the anchor crane. Then we put them to bed

By evening the wind was rising in the NW., and the glass fell rapidly. We began to take in royals. Soon we were in the middle of an electric storm, with continuous sheet lightning

We drove SE. across the mouth of the Bass Strait at 12 knots on the first leg of the 5,000-mile run to the Horn

By March 20 we were sw. of New Zealand in 49°s.,
running the easting down. It rained and rained

It was cold, too, and at the wheel and lookout we prayed
to be relieved

(*Right*) Going aloft to furl the main lower topgallant

The starboard watch mustered

On March 24, thirteen days out, we crossed the 180th meridian in 51°s. The wind was WNW., Force 6 with a heavy sea. At 5.30 the following morning we took in the upper topgallants. Big seas were coming aboard; the main deck was inundated. By noon *Moshulu* had sailed 296 miles in 23½ hours. It was the best day's run with cargo in her she ever made for Erikson

In the port watch I was given the job of looking after the four pigs who lived in styes forward by the fo'c'sle head. The crew used to paint them various brilliant colours. They spent most of their time on deck and made a terrible mess. 'Dose brodders of yours' the Mate said

(*Overleaf*) Making fast the main upper topsail. Wind wsw., Force 9. The glass fell to 733 millimetres

We took in the mizzen and main courses in heavy hail with the wind
wsw., Force 8

There were two men at the wheel constantly now

It was damp and cold in the fo'c'sles and the best place
to be was in one's bunk

Making fast mizzen upper topsail
Wind Force 9

Wind wsw., Force 10, 51°s., 158°w., carrying foresail
and lower topsails. The Captain looks aloft from the
bridge deck. There were huge following seas

The biggest seas in the world—great black walls of water, a quarter of a mile apart, as high as a three-storey house

She was running 10 knots in the biggest seas I had ever seen. The noise was indescribable—the shrieking of the wind in the shrouds, the clanging of freeing ports and the thunder of the sea as it came over the rail, like a mill race

Huge seas were coming aboard; but we still went on chipping rust below, suspended on platforms over one of the 'tween deck hatches, using oil lamps for illumination

Wind Force 11. Main and bridge decks inundated.
Seen from the main yardarm
(*Right*) The height of the gale. Foredeck seen from
the fore royal yard

Looking aft from foreyard arm, noon March 26, wind wsw., Force 11, 51°s., 158°w

Apprentice going aloft to overhaul buntlines in the main rigging

By noon on March 26 the storm entered its last phase. In spite of it we had run 228 miles in 23½ hours. Now the barometer rose steadily. All through the afternoon we were re-setting sail. At two o'clock the following morning we re-set the royals. Although the wind was falling there was still a tremendous sea running

On Easter Sunday twenty-nine days out from Port Victoria in 56°s., 74°w., when we were close-hauled on the starboard tack, we sighted a barque about 15 miles away on the port beam and to leeward of us. It was *Passat* which had left Port Lincoln two days before us. She was carrying upper topgallants but the mainsail was furled and our Captain ordered the royals to be set. Captain Lindvall of *Passat* immediately set royals, mainsail and topmast staysails. By four in the afternoon she disappeared from view in a squall and we saw her no more

There was an interval of a day, then it blew hard from WNW. and NW. Between midnight on Tuesday, March 28 and midnight on the 29th she logged 297 miles with the wind Force 6 to 8. She ran 114 miles between noon and 8 p.m., 29 of them in the first two hours of the afternoon, at times running 15 knots with the lee rail underwater, and in full sail. From noon to 4 p.m. she ran 57 miles. At 4.0 the wind freshened to Force 7 and the royals came in; at 6.0 we took in the upper topgallants with the wind Force 8, and at 7 p.m. the lower topgallants and the mizzen course, and at 4 a.m. on the 30th all hands took in the mainsail. It was the toughest, coldest night of the voyage and the Captain issued rum to all hands, using a big wooden spoon

In nine days *Moshulu* sailed 2,450 sea miles always to the south of the 51st parallel. It was very cold now but we saw no icebergs. On the 10th of April, Bank Holiday Monday, 30 days out, having sailed 6,464 sea miles, we passed the longitude of Cape Horn, in 56°s., and sighted the Diego Ramirez group. Two days more and we were by the Falkland Islands. Here Filimon and Fabian, the survivors of the five pigs who joined us at Port Victoria, round Cape Horn

A week after rounding the Horn the weather grew warmer and we began to bend fair weather canvas. On the night of April 20 it blew SSE., Force 9; the lower topsail sheet parted and the sail blew out. It then blew SSW., Force 10. The starboard watch was on deck for eleven hours. On the morning of the 22nd, at three in the morning, when the port watch had worn the ship on to the starboard tack in torrential rain the ship was struck by a Pampero, a fearful wind from the SW. which came off the South American coast, and the fore upper topgallant blew out. That day, in 28°S., 30°W., we picked up the South-East Trades which blew for ten days, losing them 4°S. South of the Line, in the Doldrums

In the Doldrums we swam

Twenty-five days from the Horn and 55 from Port Victoria we crossed the Equator in 29°w. We still had the chance to make a record passage and beat *Parma's* 1933 voyage of 83 days. She had been 30 days to the Horn, 26 to the Line, and 27 to Falmouth. We caught a shark but it straightened the iron hook that the Donkeyman had made and got away

North of the Line the winds were baffling until we picked up the North-East Trades in 5°N.; they blew for twelve days between Force 2 and 3 and then left us wallowing, seventy days out in 31°N., 47°w. on the outward extremities of the Sargasso Sea. In the next four days we only sailed 266 miles. On May 23 we only logged 10 miles between noon and 8 p.m. Mates and Captain were equally bad-tempered

Seventy-five days out we began to see some shipping. One of the steamers, *Brasilien*, reported us to Lloyd's. On the 25th and 26th the wind strengthened from the sw., Force 3 to 4 but on the 28th and 29th we encountered baffling headwinds. The 30th and 31st of May and the morning of the 1st June were good with the wind se. Force 4 to 5, but by the afternoon of the 1st the wind had died away and on the 2nd we were barely making steerage way. In five days we only sailed 235 miles. On June 5 we sailed 15 miles. Finally on June 7, the wind came back from ne. and later n., when we were about 150 miles from Queenstown and we made 9 knots on the port tack. The fore royal blew out at five in the afternoon

At 8 p.m. on June 8 we raised the Fastnet, 15 miles to the NE., but the wind fell away and we were becalmed all that night and the next day. At five in the morning of the 10th the wind went to wsw., and we squared away for Queenstown. At eleven we took the pilot and came into the anchorage in the outer roads. We were first home in ninety-one days, and although we did not know it we had made the fastest passage of the year

The starboard watch posed for a photograph

Some girls came out from the shore and the port watch celebrated
their victory